Sheepwash

Reflections of a Village

May Day parade

Margaret Waddingham

ACKNOWLEDGEMENTS

My very grateful thanks to all those people of Sheepwash who supplied material towards the compilation of this book.

An Obelisk Limited Edition

First published in 1996
Reprinted in 1997 and 1998 by
Obelisk Publications, 2 Church Hill, Pinhoe, Exeter, Devon

Ask a tourist to describe a Devon village and they will probably unwittingly describe Sheepwash – cob cottages, thatched roofs, roses round the doors and the occasional enticing glimpse of distant humps of moorland. For Sheepwash is the epitome of a Devonshire village – a picture postcard sort of place that even the dullest day can't spoil. It looks quiet and serene as though the centuries haven't touched it; a pleasant little backwater where nothing much has ever happened.

But things are rarely what they seem. For such a small village it has a great deal of history. However, it's up to you to search for the clues as it isn't the sort of place that drops large hints about its early past.

Start near the bridge at the bottom of Sheepwash Hill and look up towards the village. There you will see on your right a series of long, narrow fields. These are the original outlines laid down in feudal days when an open field system of agriculture prevailed. Some authorities think these are the most perfect remaining specimens in England. Known as 'The Sheepwash Strips', or locally as 'South Commons', they have collected another name over the years, given by the visiting fishing fraternity who struggle over rather too many stiles for comfort when loaded down with rods and nets. They call it 'The Aintree Run'.

Now come back into the village and to the Church of St Lawrence where there is a wonderful Norman font. Pause in the square at the entrance to the rear of the Half Moon and take a look at the right hand stone pillar. This is one of the surviving market pillars. Look at The Glebe in West Road and see above the porch a plaque set in the wall. It is believed to be one of a pair from those ancient market pillars.

And what about the name 'Sheepwash'? Perhaps that is the oldest thing about the village. It is said to have been derived from an Anglo-Saxon word, Schepewast, which, roughly translated, meant 'surrounded by water'. This is difficult to substantiate but what is certain is that the spelling underwent various changes throughout the centuries.

1166 Schepewast
1184 Sepewais
1253 Schepwayse
1276 Shepwaysse
1346 Schipwaysche
1358 Shiepwaysshe
1591 Shipwaishe
1675 Shipwash

– all of which came to mean 'a place to wash sheep'. Sheep there were in plenty – a fact mentioned in Domesday – but, although they are no longer washed here, the present day version of the name is at least easy to spell.

Aerial view of village with Sheepwash Strips at top

Manorial History

At the time of Domesday, Sheepwash was included in the Wessex Royal Manor of Shebbear and belonged to Torre Abbey. Ecclesiastically it was a chapelry of Shebbear until the 19th century and records show that the high alter of what was then the chapel of St Lawrence was consecrated in 1338.

Corner of Square with the former White Hart on right

During the reign of Henry I, the entire village belonged to William Fitz-Reginald, whose daughter married an Avenell. This family held it until around 1314 when it was passed to Sir Andrew Metsted. His daughter married into the Holland family, which owned the village until the reign of Charles I, at which time it was passed on to Baron Clinton.

The Market

It is difficult to imagine Sheepwash as the thriving market centre it once was. It was granted a charter in 1230 by Nicholas Avenell, and fairs with their attendant markets were held on 10 April, 10 August and 9 October each year. Because of this market Sheepwash was regarded as one of the most important centres in North Devon and continued so until 1743 when fire swept through the village and destroyed much of it. Just how much isn't really known. Some reports say that the village lay in decline for ten years, but who's to know whether one report is simply a copy of another? What is certain is that the market and its accompanying business went to Hatherleigh and Holsworthy. Although it eventually returned to the village, it never quite regained its previous fame. It operated each Monday until the end of the 18th century, along with two annual fairs, one on the second Thursday in March and the other on the first Thursday in October. Then it seemed to die out again, a smaller monthly market returning for a while during the 19th century and once again in the 1920s. It took place, as it always had done, in the farmyard at the rear of The Half Moon Inn, with the stock held in the surrounding fields.

Within living memory, this monthly market day was as hectic as it must always have been. Drovers, who sometimes took a fortnight to reach the village, picked up two head of cattle here, one there, eventually ending up with as many as 30. Some drove sheep or pigs, others drove geese. One elderly lady recalls clearly that from the age of nine she regularly drove a flock of geese from her home in Hatherleigh. By the end of the day the square and the streets leading into it were ankle deep in a rich mixture of mud and dung.

On these market days, the estate lawyer sat in the dining room of the Half Moon to collect rents, but later moved into the Tap Room (today the fireplace end of the bar) where he would sit on a big wooden settle to keep the draught off his feet. The farmers and cottagers who queued up to pay their rent would take the opportunity of making requests for repairs to their buildings. This inn, not surprisingly, did very well on such days.

The auction itself took place behind the inn, with the auctioneer sheltering from the weather beneath a large umbrella.

Market day traffic

The market eventually died out in the 1950s, its demise this time final and brought about by something as simple as progress. People were no longer driving their stock on foot and new restrictions came into being concerning transportation, not just the size of the lorries but also the cleansing of them between each load. Unfortunately Sheepwash and the lanes leading to it were far too small to cope with such innovations and the market is now little more than a memory and a few faded photographs.

In earlier days, the square would have been a little larger than it is now as there would have been no road to slice it up. The house immediately opposite the door of the inn encroaches well into the square and it is believed that this was a market house. This was rescued from years of neglect and dilapidation some time in the first half of the 19th century. The Archives say that by 1822 'the great market hall was in ruins and the material from it taken away and used by the villagers in other buildings.' It's tantalising that no-one can say exactly where this was.

The Cottages

A large number of the cottages are mid-18th century, built of cob and thatch and all very much alike, presumably because they were all rebuilt at about the same time after the great fire. Some have been found to contain charred beams, probably rescued from the original dwellings.

As the village had been owned by a succession of landlords, the cottages were not particularly well maintained. The thatched roofs were rotten and sparse and walls

Looking down South Street

were streaked with green veins of damp. It was not a rich area and many of those who did not work on the landlord's estate were small-time farmers in their own right whose fields were dotted about in such an inconvenient way that several herds of cows crisscrossed the square four times a day for milking. Even the Half Moon was an 82-acre farm, the inn being purely incidental to it. Add to this traffic the mess of the monthly market and the result was not at all the postcard image that it presents today. In fact, as recently as 1968, with the market finished and most of the homes up for sale for the first time, many cottages lay derelict and a local councillor was quoted on more than one occasion as saying that the village was like 'slum alley'. Some villagers, finding that they could not afford the price tags put on the houses that they had rented for so long, moved to the newly-built council houses in East Street and only gradually were the cottages bought and brought back to life, often by people from outside the village.

East Street opposite the Church

The oldest house is probably The Glebe, first mention of which was made in 1746 at which time it was a malt house. Although the other dwellings have no particular historical or architectural interest, it slowly began to dawn on people that here was an entire village containing some of the finest examples of thatch and cob in Devon. In 1976, and not a moment too soon, it was made a conservation area.

St Lawrence Church

The delightful church of St Lawrence is believed to be the third on the site since the 14th century, the first having fallen down and the second having burnt down. The present one was rebuilt in 1880 by Lord Clinton at a cost of £1600, and is built of stone in the early English style, consisting of a vestry and organ chamber, nave and south porch. The western tower, embattled and pinnacled, was completed in 1889 at a cost of £300, the stone with which it was built having been presented by Lord Clinton.

The east windows are beautifully stained and are the oldest in the church, presented in memory of the Cooper family. The chancel has a hammer beam roof decorated with figures of angels holding trumpets. In the south wall there are two sedilia (stone seats for priests), whilst at the back of the church is the Norman font mounted on a stone and cement pedestal. The register of baptisms dates from the year 1873 and for burials and marriages from 1675. It had the benefice of a curacy annexed to the vicarage of Shebbear.

Extension of churchyard in early '50s – The Rev Bolt and parishioners

Much of the furnishing of the church was presented by a Sheepwash benefactor, a Major Collis. It was he who provided the money for the reredos, the beautiful stained glass east windows, the solid oak lectern in the form of an eagle, and the pulpit carved with Moses holding the ten commandments and Christ depicted as the lamb of God. He also started a bell fund with a generous cheque for £250. Six bells were paid for and hung within the year of the tower's completion at a cost of £360, each bell bearing an inscription from the 65th psalm.

The new obelisk, 1920

The reredos is handsomely decorated with a painting of the Epiphany; the three kings and the Virgin Mary and child shown against a background of stars shining in the midnight air. On the alter itself there is another fine painting in oils, showing five saints, including St Lawrence himself who is holding the grid iron upon which he was burnt alive. This was painted by the wife of the Reverend Weaver, one of the past vicars.

The crocheted alter cloth was handmade in 1936 by the last schoolmistress, Mrs Taylor, who presented it to the church just before the school closed.

On each side of the alter are two chairs, one for the bishop, the other for Major Collis himself who read the lessons.

The designs of the windows in the main body of the church were selected from a catalogue, which gave a choice of kings and bishops.

The Glebe

The belfry screen, also given by Major Collis, deserves close scrutiny for its carvings of nails, hammer, sword, ladder, chisel and pincers, which depict the crucifixion, might otherwise be missed.

The organ was bought second-hand by the Reverend Wiley from Scotland. It was installed in Sheepwash in memory of Major Collis to replace the original harmonium, and the villagers subscribed to its cost of £30. The organ was hand pumped but later an electric pump was donated at a cost of £100.

Baptist Chapel

The Baptist chapel in East Street was inspired in a fit of anger in 1826. The vicar of the parish at the time was given to wining rather too well and he glided down the aisle of the church one Sunday, just managed to mount the pulpit without mishap, and announced in sad, gurgling tones, "Like an owl in the ivy bush, that woeful bird am I!"

Mrs Guest, the wife of the local excise officer, marked her disapproval by walking out of the church, vowing to build a chapel on land of her own. This she did, endowing it so that the interest should keep the building in repair.

The Bible Christian Chapel

This stands on the site of an old malt house and opened in August 1866.

Village Hall

This was built originally as a hall for meetings of the Foresters and was built in 1878.

Sheepwash Bridge, The Bridgeland Trust and the Baptism Pool

The kink in the river at the bottom of the hill had been a convenient fording place for centuries until the only son of a gentleman by the name of John Tosbury was drowned there in a sudden spate. He was so devastated at his loss that he dedicated money to build a bridge. The income from his farms and lands being more than enough to maintain this, he instructed trustees to be appointed in 1695 to see that the surplus was used for the benefit of the people of Sheepwash. This became known as the Bridgeland Trust and, although responsibility for the upkeep of the bridge was passed to Devon County Council several decades ago, to this day the income provides money for deserving cases of hardship, the upkeep of the church and chapel, outings for children and pensioners and a Christmas box for the elderly.

Sheepwash Bridge

The original bridge, with the addition of a fifth arch after heavy flooding during 1903, still stands, shuddering under the stress of 20th century traffic, but a tribute to those builders of long ago.

Looking downstream and left of the dry arch of the bridge, there was a deep pool used up to the early part of this century as a baptism pool. Good Friday was the traditional day for such occasions and the baptismal candidates, the congregation of the Baptist Chapel, as well as quite a few sightseers, would make their way down the hill to the river, singing hymns as they went. The Minister and his Deacon would lead the candidates to Bridge Cottage opposite the pool and they would emerge a few moments later barefooted and without their outer layer of clothing. For such a chilly corner of the year, total immersion was surprisingly popular.

Population

The population has risen and declined dramatically since 1800 when it numbered 348. By 1850 it had risen to 525 but by 1921 had dropped to 261. A further drop by 1951 brought it to 223 which isn't that many more than the present tally of 183 adults and approximately 30 children.

Where did they all go to? It's the usual story – many moved into towns chasing work, whilst some families simply died out. A surprising number emigrated to America and Australia.

The Dame School, now part of The Half Moon

A glance through Kelly's Directories for the mid-late 19th centuries shows just what a self-sufficient place Sheepwash was. Amongst the trades and professions mentioned were two blacksmiths, wheelwright, boot and shoe makers (four of them at one time), carpenters, two victuallers – one for the Half Moon, the other for the White Hart, farmers, an inland revenue officer, tailors, a surgeon, millers, a plumber, painter and glazier, butcher, draper, schoolmistress, stone masons, thatcher, a number of shop keepers, cooper and a milliner and bonnet maker.

Certain families were very prominent on these lists. Amongst them were William and Arthur Southcombe who were the village tailors in 1850. By 1866 Arthur had become the parish clerk and receiver at the Post Office (letters from Highampton arriving at 8.45 a.m. were dispatched at 4.20 p.m.). He was at the same time still on record as being a tailor, whilst another of the family, a Mrs Mary Southcombe, was the milliner and bonnet maker. The family must eventually have died out or moved away as there are no Southcombes left in the village today.

Associations with the Gloving Industry

Since the first half of the 16th century, the nearby town of Torrington had been connected with the manufacture of gloves as a by-product of the wool trade. In fact, it attained an enviable reputation in the trade of 'gloves superfluous', later to be known as 'gloves dainty'. At some stage, many of these gloves were sent to outlying villages as a cottage industry, Sheepwash being one of them.

Some time in the 1830s, another member of the Southcombe family, Richard (nephew to William and Arthur), became familiar with the trade as he watched the women of the village using their 'glove engines' by their cottage doors. In 1847 he moved to the village of Stoke Cross in Somerset where he set up a small factory in a shed at the back of his house. That infant firm is now one of the largest glove makers in Europe.

For a short time in the early part of this century, Sheepwash village hall was used as a glove factory by Vaughan & Co of Torrington. Between 20 and 30 young women worked there with machinery that ran from an oil engine. When it closed gloves still remained a cottage industry around Sheepwash for many years and to this day there are several people who played a part in it and who can remember glove shapes being brought out to Sheepwash from Great Torrington in a pony and trap driven by a man called Diggy Pinkham. Diggy, a bit of an opportunist, was always accompanied by a greyhound that was sent over the hedges to catch rabbits.

Sheepwash Pubs

In 1795 there were four pubs in Sheepwash: the George Inn, the White Hart where cock fighting took place, the Half Moon, which was originally three houses, and the New Inn. By 1921 there were the Clinton Arms (just around the corner from the Half Moon), the White Hart, which stood on the corner of East Street, and the Half Moon. By the turn of the century only the Half Moon remained and this surely must hold some unique record in that it has only had five landlords this century.

North Street with the former Clinton Arms on right

The square as it is today

Schools

That part of the Half Moon Inn nearest to the road was once a dame school. This was succeeded in 1873 by a purpose-built school next to the church (now a private dwelling house). The plans for this school were drawn up by Samuel Hooper of Hatherleigh who later found local fame by climbing Mount Vesuvius.

There are several people still living in the village who have very clear memories of this school in the 1920s and '30s. There were two rooms, one for the juniors, whose ages ranged between four and a half and eight, and one for the seniors of eight to fourteen, with one teacher for each.

Pupils at the village school, early '30s

In the winter, the children would often take a pasty for lunch, which they heated up in a large, black stove. Market days were favourites and as their playground abutted market fields, they would climb over the wall to join in. The school closed in 1936 and part of its playground was used to extend the adjoining graveyard. During the war it opened again for a short time for evacuees.

Lord Clinton had originally given the site for this school but accompanied it with a deed saying that it should go back to the donor if it should ever be sold. However, when it closed in 1936 he said he didn't want it and gave it to the church who sold it so that they could use it as a youth club. After that it was sold privately.

The Railway that Wasn't

Round about 1928 it was proposed to bring a railway to Sheepwash. The prospect was greeted with enthusiasm and, for a time, things looked very promising. However, things didn't go quite according to plan. The farmers and Lord Clinton all wanted a high price for their land and, while they were wasting time trying to negotiate a satisfactory price, Halwill stepped in and offered land to the railways for nothing. The railway company found it too good an opportunity to miss. The little branch line that picked up main line trains ran from Halwill to Barnstaple and the course of its track is still clearly visible where it crisscrossed the countryside. Sections of it now form part of the Tarka Trail.

The Obelisk

The Cornish granite obelisk in the centre of the square was unveiled on 23 July 1920 in honour of those from the village who died in the First World War. Forty-nine from Sheepwash served; five did not return. During the Second World War, twelve men served and one did not return. The names of all six men are inscribed on the obelisk.

The Half Moon

Of the three houses that used to form this building, the one nearest the road was a dame school, established in 1814, the middle one was a milliner's shop and the top part the inn itself.

For a long time the inn had belonged to the Clinton family. In 1921 the following advertisement appeared in a local newspaper.

> TO BE LET by tender from Michaelmas 1921, on a yearly tenancy, all that desirable free house known as 'Half Moon Hotel', situate in the village of Sheepwash, together with 65 acres of rich meadow, pasture, arable and orchard land, and, if desired, excellent salmon and trout fishing from Westover boundary to Sheepwash bridge, extending to upwards of one mile. The house contains 8 bedrooms, dining-room, private and public bars, taproom, kitchen, cellars and offices, and there are capital outbuildings, mostly slated, comprising stable accommodation for 10 horses and cattle sheds for 30 bullocks, carriage houses, cart shed, piggery, barn granary and lofts, etc., and good detached cattle and sheep sheds. There is an excellent monthly market held on the premises which is distant about six and a half miles from Halwill Junction Railway Station.

At that stage, and indeed up to the time the market finally disappeared, the yard at the back of the inn was all part of the farm. The four bedrooms now known as 'The Stable Block' was originally stabling, as was The Badger House, whose garden was a collecting yard for store cattle on market day. Once a year sheep dipping took place there, an exercise which required the services of a policeman to oversee it. The Shippon used to be cow sheds and stores and in more recent times, was used for farrowing pigs.

The current owners, the Inniss family, arrived in 1958. At this time the thatch at the yard end of the building had been removed and replaced by shingle by the previous landlord, but the inn was still quite small.

The Rod Room used to be a kitchen, which had an inconvenient outside bulge of a cloam oven that got in the way of the beer lorries so had to be removed. The bar itself was originally three separate rooms; the present carpeted area being the snug, the centre part the tiny bar and the top end by the fireplace the tap room. The present kitchen was more stabling. The location of the dining room hasn't changed but was only half the size of the present one. During some of the inside work in 1959, an ancient fire stone and a fishpond ash catcher made of pottery were discovered.

Gradually Ruth and the Wing Commander (known to all as Bree) Inniss, with the help of their second son, Benjie, began to make changes. When Ruth died suddenly in the early '70s, the youngest son, Charles, came to join the firm and today it is Benjie and Charles who are joint owners of the Half Moon. At the time of writing this, the inn has been in the continuous ownership of one family for nearly 40 years and visitors come to enjoy its friendly welcome from all over the world.

Reverend Roberts

It is hard, when writing a history of a place like this, not to mention at least one of the characters who, in his own unique way, contributed to it. The Reverend Roberts arrived in Sheepwash in the mid-1950s. He was a colourful personality who had enlisted at the age of 16 with the Royal Welsh Fusiliers during the First World War and fought on the Somme and at Arras. During the civil war of 1918 between the Red and the White Russians, he was drafted into the North Russian Expeditionary Force sent out by the government to intervene on behalf of the Whites. There he was taken prisoner and spent nine months in a Moscow gaol where he kept a minute diary, remarkable not only for its full eye-witness account of the fighting and the ensuing incarceration, but also for its size. It measured a mere three inches by two and a half inches and contained 70,000 words, microscopic but quite legible with the aid of a magnifying glass.

Reverend Roberts was a man of great fighting spirit and he spent a considerable amount of time and energy writing letters to newspapers on all manner of subjects ranging from nuclear disarmament to better conditions for the clergy. But he was a man who got things done. Whilst in the village, all six bells were re-hung, heating was installed in the church and he founded the Sheepwash Singers who, for a few years, gave concerts all over Devon and Cornwall.

He was always surprising his parishioners, but he shook them to their very roots when, at the age of about 70, he answered an advert in one of the more dubious Sunday papers, and offered his services to a young lady who wanted to find the ideal man to father her child. Maybe because of his age, or maybe because of his profession, Reverend Roberts made it to the short list and, amongst a few other lucky candidates, went up to a London hotel to meet the young lady. So far as we know, there the matter ended. Whether she turned him down or the other way round, it appears that he didn't make the finals.

Samuel Johnson's Diary

There is in the village a wonderful diary covering the years 1862/1869. It is particularly remarkable in that it records, not his own life as one would imagine, but the life and happenings of those around him. By doing so the writer has left a vivid account of the day-to-day lives of the people of Sheepwash at that time.

There are accounts of Vestry Meetings in the White Hart to choose Parish Officers and meetings in the Half Moon to choose three constables for the year.

It tells of burials, marriages and of confinements for births, both legitimate and illegitimate.

It tells of deaths, timely and otherwise; of a baby who died swallowing a nut 'with his shell and all the contents', and the child who drowned whilst his father was at Highampton horse racing. Of a man killed by his own bull and another who 'suffered death by cart upset'.

It tells of women who died in childbirth – sadly a large number of these – and the entries usually ended with such words as 'leaving her husband with five girls to lament her'.

Details of the people who left the village for Australia, America and New Zealand are recorded. Sometimes the name of the ship on which they sailed, together with the number of passengers, was given, and the entries followed up several months later with notes about the money – usually £5 or £10 – that was sent home to their families at regular intervals and where it was to be cashed.

Sometimes the entries help to give a background to events. The railways, for instance, had evidently been planned long before the 1920s, because the diary tells us that 'the commencement of taking the levels for the railway by Sheepwash was something in the time of 1864 in the months of May, June or July or near that time. I cannot say the certain date.' A further entry in 1866 records the visit of a land surveyor for the Mid-Devon Railway Company who came in April to commence valuation of the land for the railways.

Bank Villas, North Street, now the site of two modern houses

In May 1864 a surveyor from North Tawton came for the first time to survey the highways of Sheepwash, whilst in April of the following year, a contract was signed for taking the highway to Sheepwash.

On 7 September 1865, the foundation stone was laid for the Bible Christian Chapel in the garden of the malthouse. The commencement of taking down this malthouse by Mr Rowlands's labourers was in July 1866 and only one month later the Chapel opened, attended by a choir and many speakers.

Now and then there are interesting snippets of news from neighbouring towns like these:

The new Magistrate rooms at Hatherleigh opened on 20 December 1864.

The Tavistock–Launceston railway opened on 1 July 1865.

The Bideford Commercial Bank stopped payments in May 1866.

Occasionally, he recorded national happenings, like the marriage of the Prince of Wales to Princess Alexandra or the death of Lord Palmerston in 1865. Or, perhaps closer to a countryman's heart, 'the cattle plague was very heavy in many parts in England in 1865 and 1866 but not very heavy in Devonshire.'

Crimes in Sheepwash were faithfully noted. The first two prisoners to be confined in the new Hatherleigh Magistrate Rooms were given one month each for taking barley. In 1862 a certain William Mandock took the writer's watch and, for some reason unspecified, 'broke it to pieces'. For this he was committed at Hatherleigh Petty Sessions. In 1866 his name crops up again for not supporting his family. He was again committed, this time at the Black Torrington Petty Sessions, to three weeks hard labour.

In 1863 a Charles Smale was committed to one month at Exeter Gaol for deserting his wife and children and in the same year Richard Sanders was brought before the magistrates for stealing turnips but was discharged. Mr William Isaac had an order against him for an illegitimate child for 2/- (10 pence) a week, and all expenses.

Here too are the ordinary and less ordinary events that surrounded the lives of the people of Sheepwash.

'We had a great landwater (flood) on Sunday, 14 September 1862.'

'A ploughing match was held near Merton on the property of Lord Clinton 11 December 1862.'

'23 January 1863 Mrs Newcombe received news of the death of her brother in India who died on 10 December 1862.'

'A ball took place at Great Torrington for the great gentlemen of rank on 9 February 1863.'

'The Gloving Master died at Great Torrington on 21 February 1863.'

'William Johnson bought his second pig for 14/- (70 pence) on 23 October 1865.'

'Horse races came off at Sheepwash on 8 September 1865 and Mrs Madge's mare won the goblet for the flat race. '

There was mention of singing meetings at the Half Moon, harvest homes, parties with bread and cake for the charity children at the school, the death of a tinker and another death of someone who had 'a sad accident with a roller', a visit of The Riders from a circus in Hatherleigh. Accounts of visits of friends and family to the village, and records of the names of people who left it to seek employment elsewhere, like Grace May who, in April 1865 went for service with someone in Bideford, and someone else who went as a porter to a London station.

There is an account of a sermon preached in Sheepwash church in aid of the Pastoral Church Society. This entry not only records the date, but the name of the preacher and even the text for the sermon.

There were touches of sadness. William Dark was brought back from Plympton from the asylum on 20 December 1865 and a lady was taken after her confinement to an asylum in Salisbury. A Miss Short was taken by the relieving officer at Sheepwash to the blind school at Exeter on Boxing Day, 1865.

The diary is in copperplate handwriting and written in the colloquial language of the day. Much of it is faded and difficult to read; some entries are even written one on top of the other, but for an accurate record of the past and a feeling that there still remains a living link with the history of Sheepwash, it is hard to beat.

Women's Institute meeting in the '50s